I0817097

CORE LIBRARY OF US STATES

ALABAMA

BY MARCIA AMIDON LUSTED

CONTENT CONSULTANT
Ruth Truss, PhD
Professor of History
University of Montevallo

Core Library

An Imprint of Abdo Publishing
abdobooks.com

abdobooks.com

Published by Abdo Publishing, a division of ABDO, PO Box 398166, Minneapolis, Minnesota 55439.

Printed in the United States of America, North Mankato, Minnesota.
052022
092022

Cover Photo: Shutterstock Images
Interior Photos: Shutterstock Images, 4–5, 26–27, 34–35, 43; Red Line Editorial, 9 (Alabama), 9 (USA); Sarin Images/Granger Historical Picture Archive, 10–11; T. Lesia/Shutterstock Images, 13 (flag); Danté Fenolio/Science Source, 13 (salamander); Fiona M. Donnelly/Shutterstock Images, 13 (bird); Janina Zilys/Shutterstock Images, 13 (flower); Billy Fam/iStockphoto, 13 (tree); North Wind Picture Archives/AP Images, 15; Universal History Archive/Universal Images Group/Getty Images, 18; Rob Hainer/Shutterstock Images, 20–21, 45; Ryan M. Bolton/Shutterstock Images, 22; George Dodd III/ Shutterstock Images, 29; JSC/NASA, 37; Sean Pavone/Shutterstock Images, 38

Editor: Angela Lim
Series Designer: Joshua Olson

Library of Congress Control Number: 2021951395

Publisher's Cataloging-in-Publication Data

Names: Lusted, Marcia Amidon, author.
Title: Alabama / by Marcia Amidon Lusted
Description: Minneapolis, Minnesota : Abdo Publishing, 2023 | Series: Core library of US states | Includes online resources and index.
Identifiers: ISBN 9781532197420 (lib. bdg.) | ISBN 9781098270186 (ebook)
Subjects: LCSH: U.S. states--Juvenile literature. | Southeastern States--Juvenile literature. | Alabama--History--Juvenile literature. | Physical geography--United States--Juvenile literature.
Classification: DDC 976.1--dc23

Population demographics broken down by race and ethnicity come from the 2019 census estimate. Population totals come from the 2020 census.

CONTENTS

USA
SKYLAB

CHAPTER ONE

THE HEART OF DIXIE

A cluster of tall, white rockets points toward the sky. A mounted space shuttle with solid rocket boosters looks like it's flying through the air. Visitors head inside to explore the museum. They look at moon rocks and the very first US satellite, *Explorer I*. A group of students there for Space Camp are learning about a Project Mercury spacecraft.

All of these things are happening at the US Space and Rocket Center in the city of

A Saturn V rocket is on display at the US Space and Rocket Center in Huntsville, Alabama.

Huntsville, Alabama. The city is nicknamed Rocket City. It has been a part of the US space program for 60 years. The Marshall Space Flight Center is nearby. This center is run by the National Aeronautics and Space Administration (NASA). Space technology and equipment is built and tested there. Huntsville itself is an exciting city with many things to do and see. There are concerts, art galleries, and museums. There's even a Secret Art Trail to explore.

ABOUT ALABAMA

Alabama is in the southeastern region of the United States. Tennessee borders it to the north and Georgia to the east. Florida forms its southern border. Mississippi lies to the west. Alabama also touches the Gulf of Mexico to the south.

Alabama does not have an official nickname. But it is sometimes called the Heart of Dixie. Dixie is the nickname for the American South. And Alabama sits right in the middle, or in the heart, of the Deep South.

The origin of this nickname may go back to the 1800s when Louisiana, another Southern state, began printing *dix*, the French word for "ten," on its $10 banknotes.

Montgomery is Alabama's capital. It is located in the south-central part of the state. Birmingham has the largest population. Other major cities include Huntsville, near the Tennessee border, and Mobile, on the Gulf Coast.

PERSPECTIVES

RICK BRAGG

Author Rick Bragg was born in Alabama. He won the Pulitzer Prize in 1996 for his writing in the *New York Times*. Many of his books and essays are about his family and growing up in Alabama, where he still lives. In his collection of writings *Where I Come From: Stories from the Deep South*, Bragg described the South. He wrote, "[The South] is a [long list] of great talkers, blue-green waters, deep casseroles . . . things that make this place more than a dotted line on a map or a long-ago failed rebellion."

Alabama's geography features hills and valleys in the north. It has plains to the south that reach down to Mobile Bay on the Gulf of Mexico. The state has 1,500 miles (2,400 km) of rivers and waterways. Major rivers including the Tombigbee, Black Warrior, and Coosa run through the state. Seventy percent of Alabama is covered in forests.

SO MANY NICKNAMES

Alabama may be known as the Heart of Dixie, but it has other nicknames too. It is also called the Yellowhammer State. Huntsville troops in the Civil War wore yellow patches on their uniforms. The soldiers were called yellowhammers, which is a type of bird. Today the yellowhammer, or northern flicker, is Alabama's state bird. Alabama's other nickname is the Cotton State because of its history of cotton plantations.

Alabama is a state with many beautiful and interesting places to explore. It also has a long and rich history. It has been home to many amazing people, both past and present.

MAP OF ALABAMA

Alabama has many major cities. How might landforms and bodies of water influence the landscape near these cities?

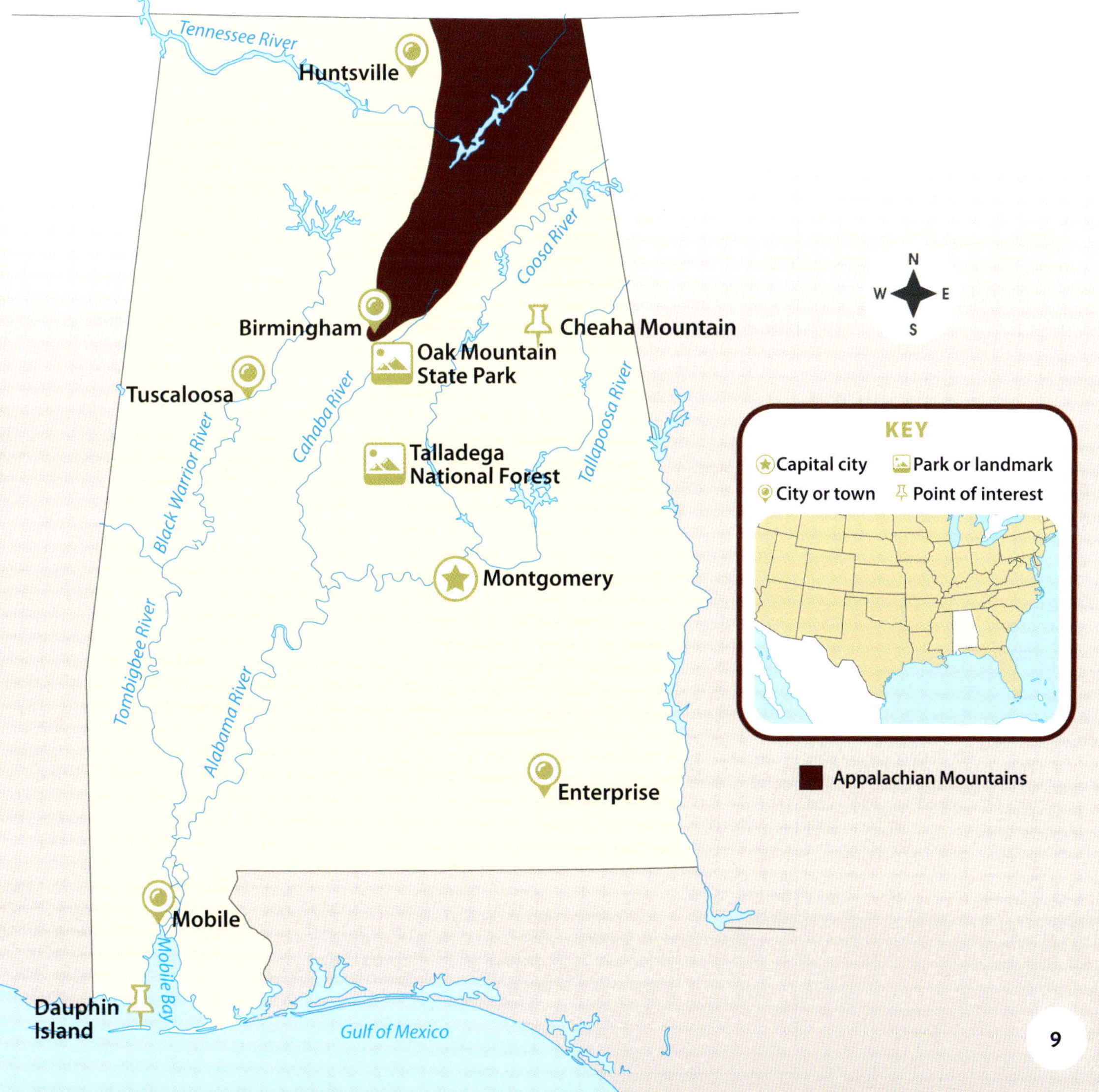

CHAPTER TWO

HISTORY OF ALABAMA

People have been living in Alabama for more than 10,000 years. The first peoples were Paleo-Indians. The Mississippian culture developed by 1000 CE. Peoples of this culture built earthen mounds that can still be seen today.

By the 1500s, many American Indian nations were established in the region. Some of these nations included the Cherokee, the Choctaw, and the Muscogee (Creek). Today Alabama officially recognizes nine American

General Andrew Jackson, *left*, met with Muscogee leader William Weatherford, *right*, in 1814.

Indian tribes. But the Poarch Band of Creeks is the only federally recognized tribe in the state.

EUROPEANS ARRIVE

The first European explorers arrived in present-day Alabama in 1519. Spanish explorer Hernando de Soto led a large expedition searching for gold in 1540. His men did not find gold, and they came into conflict with American Indian nations including the Choctaw. They killed thousands of American Indian people.

In 1702 the French built Fort Louis, the first permanent European settlement in Alabama. It was located north of what is now the city of Mobile. A 1763 treaty between Britain and France handed over the Mobile region to the British. Just two decades later, the United States won independence from Britain in the American Revolution (1775–1783). Another treaty gave the United States control over most of Alabama. It also gave the Mobile area to Spain.

ALABAMA

QUICK FACTS

Take a look at Alabama's state symbols. How do they help you understand the state's geography?

Abbreviation: AL
Nickname: The Heart of Dixie
Motto: *Audemus jura nostra defendere* (We dare maintain our rights)
Date of statehood: December 14, 1819
Capital: Montgomery
Population: 5,024,279
Area: 52,420 square miles (135,767 sq km)

STATE SYMBOLS

State amphibian
Red Hills salamander

State flower
Camellia

State bird
Yellowhammer

State tree
Longleaf pine

In 1803 the United States purchased the Louisiana Territory from France. Much of this territory is now the midwestern United States. In 1813 the US government declared that the purchase also included Mobile. It forced Spain out of the region entirely. During this period many American settlers arrived in the area. The US military battled American Indians in the region for land. The US government forced many American Indian peoples to leave. On December 14, 1819, Alabama became the twenty-second US state. The state's population at this time stood at about 128,000. More than 30 percent was enslaved.

FROM STATEHOOD TO CIVIL WAR

At the time Alabama became a state, cotton was a key crop in the South. To grow this cotton, plantation owners used labor from enslaved people. The state's enslaved population doubled in the 1820s. It doubled again in the 1830s.

An engraving from the 1800s depicts enslaved people working on a cotton plantation. Enslaved people were forced to work long hours without rest.

The cotton industry also forced American Indians from the land. In 1830 the US government passed the Indian Removal Act. The law allowed the president to handle removal treaties with nations. The US government forced many American Indians, including about 1,200 Alabama Cherokees, out of the state to make room for more cotton farms.

Tensions rose in the 1860s. Southern states left the United States beginning in 1860. These states formed the Confederacy, where slavery was legal. Alabama became the fourth state to secede on January 11, 1861.

THE *H. L. HUNLEY*

In 1863 a team of shipbuilders in Mobile began building the *H. L. Hunley* for the Confederacy. It was one of the first submarines built for war. The *H. L. Hunley* was designed to attach a mine to an enemy ship and then escape before the mine exploded. The submarine sank a Union ship near South Carolina in February 1864. But the submarine never resurfaced. Divers discovered the wreck in 1995, and it was raised to the surface in 2000. Shock waves from the mine's explosion may have killed the crew.

The northern states, called the Union, fought to keep the country together. This conflict was the Civil War. For a few months in 1861, the Confederate capital was Montgomery. It was later moved to Richmond, Virginia. The Union controlled much of northern Alabama during the war. Union troops launched attacks on the Confederacy from bases there. US Navy warships took control of Mobile Bay in August 1864. The war ended in 1865 with a Union victory. The country became whole again, and it outlawed slavery in all states.

AFTER THE CIVIL WAR

Industries in Alabama began to change after the Civil War. The state's economy started producing more goods in factories. Many people moved from the country to the cities for work.

Slavery ended after the war, but Black and white Americans were still not treated equally. Alabama and other Southern states passed rules that became known as Jim Crow laws. These made segregation legal. Segregation kept Black people separated from

PERSPECTIVES

ROSA PARKS

In 1955 Black bus riders in Montgomery had to sit in the back of the bus. They also had to give up their seats for white people if the bus was too crowded. In 1955 Rosa Parks refused to give up her seat to a white person. Parks was arrested. Her action sparked the Montgomery bus boycott. Black people avoided taking the bus for 13 months after Parks's arrest. In 1956 the US Supreme Court banned segregation on buses. Parks later said, "I would like to be remembered as a person who wanted to be free . . . so other people would be also free."

Rosa Parks attracted national attention after she refused to give up her bus seat for a white person.

white people. They had to attend different schools, enter public spaces through separate doors, and even use separate restrooms. These laws also limited voting rights.

Jim Crow laws lasted until the civil rights movement of the 1950s and 1960s. People in Alabama played an important role in the movement. Minister and activist Martin Luther King Jr. led major civil rights campaigns. The Montgomery bus boycott of 1955 and 1956 protested segregation on public transportation. King protested discrimination in Birmingham in 1963 and was jailed for eight days. In 1964 he and many other activists marched from Selma to Montgomery to push for equal voting rights. These and other events led to changes in laws and public attitudes about civil rights.

Today Alabama's government is made up of three branches. Elected officials in the legislative branch write and vote on new bills. The executive branch includes the governor, who signs bills into law. The judicial branch decides how the laws should be applied.

FURTHER EVIDENCE

Chapter Two discusses the civil rights movement in Alabama. What was one of the main points of this section? What evidence is included to support this point? Read the article at the website below. Does the information on the website support the main point of the section? Does it present new evidence?

20 PLACES THAT CHANGED THE WORLD

abdocorelibrary.com/alabama

CHAPTER THREE

GEOGRAPHY AND CLIMATE

Alabama's geography varies throughout the state. The Appalachian Mountains run through northeastern and central Alabama. Cheaha Mountain is located on the southernmost tip of the Appalachian Mountains. It is the highest point in Alabama and stands 2,413 feet (735 m) above sea level. The mountain is in the middle of Talladega National Forest, which includes chestnut oaks and Virginia pines.

Little River Canyon Preserve offers scenic views of waterfalls and wildlife.

Approximately 51 percent of the freshwater turtle species in North America, including the alligator snapping turtle, live in Alabama rivers.

Alabama's state tree, the longleaf pine, is also found there and throughout the state.

The fall line runs from the northwestern corner of Alabama to the mid-southeastern border of the state. It is formed by an abrupt change in elevation. When rivers cross the fall line, they have waterfalls. The Cahaba River is one river that crosses over the fall line. It eventually flows into the Alabama River, which empties into Mobile Bay. More types of fish live in the Cahaba River than in the entire state of California.

Plains dominate the southeastern region of the state. Swamps, including the Sipsey River Swamp, are also in the southeast. Bald cypress trees grow along this swamp, which is home to 37 types of mussels. The Red Hills salamander lives in a small region of southeastern Alabama. This rare type of salamander is Alabama's state amphibian. Alligators live in slow-moving rivers and are often found near Alabama's coasts.

PERSPECTIVES

ALABAMA'S STATE FLOWER

The camellia became Alabama's state flower in 1959. It is usually white but can be pink or red. Unlike most flowering plants, camellias bloom in the late fall and winter. The camellia was once rare in Alabama. But gardeners worked to make the flower common throughout the state. The Alabama Camellia Society celebrates the flower's beauty and history. Forrest Latta is the vice president of the society. He said, "It's like apple pie. There [isn't anybody] who doesn't like a camellia."

Alabama borders the Gulf of Mexico for 60 miles (97 km). White sands made of quartz cover Alabama's shores. Alabama's coastal region includes lagoons and islands and is a major tourist destination in the state.

CLIMATE

Different regions of Alabama experience different weather patterns. But for the most part, the state's climate is humid and warm throughout the year. Summer temperatures can be very hot, with an average temperature of more than 90 degrees Fahrenheit (32°C). Winters are mild, and snowfall is rare.

Alabama receives approximately 56 inches (142 cm) of rain every year. This amount of rainfall combined with the warm climate is good for growing crops. Alabama's growing season lasts for 300 days each year.

DAUPHIN ISLAND

Dauphin Island is a barrier island located just 3 miles (5 km) off Alabama's coast. Gulf waves leave behind soil and sand as they move toward the mainland, forming the barrier island. The waters surrounding Dauphin Island are home to many types of marine animals. Visitors can take boat tours to see dolphins. Sea turtles lay eggs on the island's shores. Dauphin Island is also home to around 350 types of birds.

The state also experiences extreme weather. Alabama is part of a region called Dixie Alley. Tornadoes are common in this region. Alabama has seen an increase in tornadoes since 1990.

Due to the state's location near the Gulf of Mexico, hurricanes and tropical storms are common. Hurricane Katrina made landfall in the United States in 2005. Water levels in Mobile Bay rose approximately 11.5 feet (3.5 m), putting many homes and businesses underwater.

EXPLORE ONLINE

Chapter Three describes some of the animals living in Alabama. The website below explores some of the state's rare animals and the threats they face. As you know, every source is different. What information does the website give about the wildlife in Alabama? How is the information from the website the same as the information in Chapter Three? What new information did you learn from the website?

ALABAMA IS HOME TO THIRD MOST ENDANGERED SPECIES IN THE NATION

abdocorelibrary.com/alabama

CHAPTER FOUR

RESOURCES AND ECONOMY

Agriculture is one of the largest industries in Alabama. Crops and livestock bring approximately $70.4 billion dollars into the state each year. Some of its top crops include cotton, soybeans, and peanuts. Alabama is a major producer of chicken, cattle, and catfish.

Timber is another part of the agricultural industry. Alabama forests stretch across 23 million acres (9.3 million ha). This is a larger area than the area of Connecticut, Delaware,

Alabama produces more than 400 million pounds (181 million kg) of peanuts each year.

BOLL WEEVILS

The boll weevil is a beetle that feeds on only cotton blossoms and buds. It arrived in the United States in 1892. Since then it has caused an estimated $23 billion in damages on US cotton farms. By 1909 the weevil was in Enterprise. At the time, cotton was the main crop in the region. Weevils feasted on the cotton. Farmers were not able to sell as much of the crop. This led Enterprise farmers to grow different plants. Agricultural production rebounded as farmers began growing peanuts, potatoes, and other crops. Today a sculpture in Enterprise features a woman holding a boll weevil. The sculpture celebrates the impact the beetle had on agriculture.

Massachusetts, New Jersey, and Rhode Island combined. Healthy soil allows trees to grow back quickly. Sawmills and paper mills transform trees into wood and paper products.

NATURAL RESOURCES AND ENERGY

US soldiers first discovered coal in Alabama in 1815. The coal mining industry grew in the 1850s. Alabama ranked tenth

Florida and Alabama meet at Perdido Key, a popular tourist destination on the Gulf of Mexico.

in the nation in coal production in 2018. Alabama does not mine as much coal as other states. But most of the coal from overseas enters through ports in Mobile.

Natural gas is the main source of energy used in the state. But the state uses other sources of energy too. Nuclear power accounts for more than 30 percent of Alabama's electricity. Nearly 9 percent comes from hydropower. And approximately 2 percent of the state's energy comes from burning wood and other plant material.

PERSPECTIVES

A HUNTING STATE

Hunting and fishing brought $3.2 billion into Alabama's economy in 2018. Much of this money came from Alabama residents. In comparison to other US states, Alabama has a long hunting season.

In recent years more women have begun taking up the sport. Amber Sanders is a hunter from Montgomery. She compared female hunters to male hunters. Sanders said, "Our camo may have some pink on the logo or around the collar, but we're just as serious as the guys. And we can outhunt the guys too."

SCIENCE AND TECHNOLOGY

Alabama's aeronautics industry extends back to 1910. That year Orville and Wilbur Wright built a flight school in Montgomery. It was the first of its kind in the United States. The Wright Brothers built the first airplane in 1903.

Today aerospace companies are located throughout the state. Marshall Space Flight Center is a major research facility for NASA. The center develops spacecraft and technology for space exploration. Scientists in Huntsville designed Saturn V. This was the rocket that allowed people to travel to the Moon. US Army pilots train at Fort Rucker. The base is 80 miles (129 km) southeast of Montgomery.

Alabama specializes in other areas of transportation too. It ranks in the top five states for automobile production. Companies including Mercedes-Benz, Toyota, and Hyundai manufacture cars and trucks in Alabama. More than 40,000 Alabama workers help produce more than 1 million vehicles each year. Alabama is also a top auto exporting state. Countries such as China, Canada, and Germany buy Alabama-made cars.

Scientific and medical advancements also occur in the state. Cummings Research Park is the second-largest research and technology park in the United States. Many companies have laboratories there. Scientists conduct studies to produce new medicine and health-care technology. Some of the Park's other industries include cybersecurity, aerospace, and defense.

In July 2020 the Alabama government established the Alabama Innovation Commission. This commission helps new business owners. Former US secretary of state Dr. Condoleezza Rice spoke of being appointed to the council:

> *Alabama is home to me, and I am honored to serve on the advisory council for the Alabama Innovation Commission. . . . This is an opportunity to create forward-thinking ideas and policies that will inspire the next generation of innovators. By focusing on knowledge-based skills and education, technology growth and entrepreneurship, we unlock the potential for future success across the state.*

Source: "Governor Ivey Announces Creation of the Alabama Innovation Commission to Promote Entrepreneurial Growth." *The Office of Alabama Governor Kay Ivey*, 16 July 2020, governor.alabama.gov. Accessed 29 June 2021.

BACK IT UP

The author of this passage is using evidence to support a point. Write a paragraph describing the point the author is making. Then write down two or three pieces of evidence the author uses to make the point.

LEADER
TREME
Jones Sr.
LEADER
REMO

CHAPTER FIVE

PEOPLE AND PLACES

Alabama was home to 5,024,279 people in 2020. More than 65 percent of the population is non-Hispanic white. Nearly 27 percent of Alabama residents are Black, and more than 4 percent are Hispanic. Asians make up less than 2 percent of the population, and less than 1 percent is American Indian.

The Treme Brass Band performed at the Mardi Gras Block Party in Montgomery in 2017.

FAMOUS ALABAMIANS

Many famous people were born in Alabama. Helen Keller was born in Tuscumbia in 1880. When she was two years old, she caught an illness that resulted in her becoming blind and deaf. She later became a speaker, author, and disability rights activist.

Harper Lee wrote the classic American novel *To Kill a Mockingbird*. Her hometown of Monroeville inspired the small-town Alabama setting of her famous novel. Other famous people from Alabama include baseball player Hank Aaron and soccer

W. C. HANDY

W. C. Handy was born in Alabama in 1873. He learned to play the cornet, an instrument similar to a trumpet. He became a professional musician and played with bands that toured the South. Handy learned about Black folk music, which is now known as the blues. He began writing his own blues songs. His songs "Saint Louis Blues" and "Memphis Blues" became hits. They helped make the music genre popular. Handy is often called the Father of the Blues.

Mae Jemison joined six other astronauts on the space shuttle *Endeavour* in September 1992.

player Mia Hamm. Astronaut Mae Jemison was born in Decatur. She became the first Black woman to travel in space.

PLACES TO VISIT

Alabama has many great places to visit. Birmingham is one of its largest cities. Visitors to the Birmingham Civil Rights Institute learn about the city's connection to the civil rights movement. The Alabama Sports Hall of Fame and Museum showcases the athletic talent

Birmingham was home to approximately 210,000 people in 2019.

from the state. Other museums spotlight Alabama's aerospace industry. The city also has theaters, parks, and award-winning restaurants.

Huntsville is another major city. It is most well-known for its NASA flight center, but its history extends back much further. Houses from before the Civil

War still stand. This includes the Weeden House, which was built in 1819.

Beach lovers enjoy Mobile. The city is located on the Gulf Coast and is known for its white sand beaches. Dauphin Island sits off the coast near Mobile. It is home to the Sea Lab, which is an aquarium and research center. Mobile's Mardi Gras celebration is the oldest in the nation. It first took place in 1703. More than 40 Mardi Gras parades happen

PERSPECTIVES

US CIVIL RIGHTS TRAIL

The US Civil Rights Trail winds through several Southern states, including Alabama. Some of the sites include the location of Rosa Parks's arrest and the church where Martin Luther King Jr. preached. The director of the Alabama Tourism Department in 2021, Lee Sentell, wrote a book about the locations along the trail. Bernice King, the daughter of Martin Luther King Jr., spoke at the book launch. She said, "It's important that families all across this nation—regardless of race, ethnicity—bring their children to these historical sites to learn the stories of brave, courageous, visionary, nonviolent individuals who changed the South forever."

in downtown Mobile each year. People in the parade throw beaded necklaces and marshmallow MoonPies.

Outdoor adventures lie away from the cities. Alabama has 24 state parks. Oak Mountain State Park is the largest. It offers views of pine-covered mountains. People enjoy hiking, fishing, and boating in the park. Russell Cave is a national monument. People from early cultures lived in the cave more than 10,000 years ago.

College football is a big deal in Alabama. Auburn University and the University of Alabama are often among the nation's best teams. Tens of thousands of fans come to each school's home games. But their biggest game is the one against each other. Nicknamed the Iron Bowl, it's often one of the most-watched games in the whole country each year.

Alabama is a state with many places to visit. It is home to a variety of wildlife. Growing industries attract people to the state. Alabama's rich history, big cities, and natural beauty make it an exciting place to visit.

STRAIGHT TO THE SOURCE

In 2021 the Alabama government made the Dauphin Island Sea Lab the official aquarium of Alabama. State representative Chip Brown worked to make it official. He said:

> *The Dauphin Island Sea Lab and its aquarium are among the state's greatest tourism treasures and have certainly earned recognition as the "Official Aquarium of Alabama." It is my hope that the title will be used to market the Sea Lab, attract more tourists and visitors, and generate additional dollars for the facility's important research work, [conservation] programs, and educational efforts.*

Source: "Legislature Declares Dauphin Island Sea Lab the 'Official Aquarium of Alabama.'" *Alabama Political Reporter*, 6 May 2021, alreporter.com. Accessed 29 May 2021.

WHAT'S THE BIG IDEA?

Take a close look at this passage. What is the main connection being made between the aquarium and tourism? What can you tell about the Sea Lab and the Alabama economy from this excerpt? What other connections does Brown make with the Sea Lab?

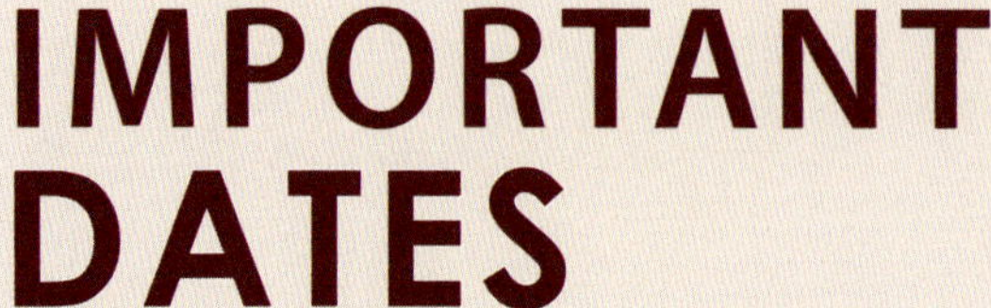

IMPORTANT DATES

10,000 years ago
The first peoples live in Alabama.

1519
The first European explorers arrive in Alabama.

1702
The French build the first permanent European settlement in Alabama at Fort Louis.

1813
The US government drives the Spanish out of the Mobile region.

1819
Alabama becomes the twenty-second US state on December 14.

1861
On January 11 Alabama becomes the fourth state to secede from the Union and join the Confederacy.

1910
Orville and Wilbur Wright build the first US flight school in Montgomery.

1955
Black residents begin boycotting Montgomery buses to protest segregation on public transportation.

1964
Martin Luther King Jr. leads a march from Selma to Montgomery for equal voting rights.

2005
Hurricane Katrina causes widespread damage in Alabama.

STOP AND THINK

Dig Deeper

After reading this book, what questions do you still have about the geography of Alabama? With an adult's help, find a few reliable sources that can help answer these questions. Write a short paragraph about what you learned.

Take a Stand

Chapter Four describes the effect the boll weevil had on Alabama agriculture. It caused severe damage to cotton crops and forced farmers to plant other crops instead of cotton. Do you think the beetle had more of a positive or negative impact on the state's agriculture? Explain your answer.

You Are There

This book describes Alabama's white sand beaches. Imagine you are taking a trip to the shores of the Gulf of Mexico. Write a letter home telling your friends about your activities on the beach. Be sure to add plenty of detail to your notes.

Another View

This book talks about Alabama during the Civil War. As you know, every source is different. Ask a librarian or another adult to help you find another source about this event. Write a short essay comparing and contrasting the point of view of the new source with that of this book. What is the point of view of each author? How are they similar and why? How are they different and why?

GLOSSARY

aeronautics
a science dealing with flight and aircraft

boycott
the act of refusing a good or service, usually as a form of protest

discrimination
when people treat others differently based on certain factors such as appearance

hydropower
electricity that is created by moving water

innovation
a new idea, method, or device

lagoon
a shallow channel or pond that connects to a larger body of water

nuclear
relating to the type of energy produced by splitting atoms; commonly associated with atomic bombs

plantation
a large farm where the workers live on-site

secede
to leave a political union

treaty
an official agreement between governments

ONLINE RESOURCES

To learn more about Alabama, visit our free resource websites below.

Visit **abdocorelibrary.com** or scan this QR code for free Common Core resources for teachers and students, including vetted activities, multimedia, and booklinks, for deeper subject comprehension.

Visit **abdobooklinks.com** or scan this QR code for free additional online weblinks for further learning. These links are routinely monitored and updated to provide the most current information available.

LEARN MORE

Buckley, James, Jr. *Helen Keller.* Portable, 2021.

Harris, Duchess, and Heather C. Hudak. *Rosa Parks Stays Seated.* Abdo, 2019.

INDEX

About the Author

Marcia Amidon Lusted has written more than 200 books and 600 magazine articles for young readers. She is an editor and also works in sustainable development around the world.